MANOPAUSE

MANOPAUSE

Boomer Hits the Big 50

Mark Poncy

VANTAGE PRESS
New York

FIRST EDITION

Copyright © 1997 by Mark Poncy

Published by Vantage Press, Inc.
516 West 34th Street, New York, New York 10001

Manufactured in the United States of America
ISBN: 0-533-12345-3

Library of Congress Catalog Card No.: 97-90295

0 9 8 7 6 5 4 3 2 1

To Marnie, because she's still funny

Contents

Contents

Foreword

This wasn't My idea. In fact, he first approached his mother, but she had the common sense to refuse.

When Mark then asked Me to write the foreword to this tiny book of his, My first response was to send a little bolt of lightning down in his vicinity. Nothing lethal, you understand, but it's been My experience that if the lightning doesn't deliver the message, the thunderclap generally gets the point across. After all, it's been almost two thousand years since I've written anything (not that anyone reads anymore), and I'll be Self-darned if I'm going to break my silence for a piddly venture like *Manopause*.

But the guy just didn't get it. He kept coming back like those little men in the electric football game, pushing relentlessly forward in that numbskull fashion of his. So I started thinking about it, and came to the conclusion that if it would make him go away, it might not be such a bad deal to get out the old tablet and etch a few words.

You humans are imbued with a sense of time, a little trick I cooked up to keep you interested in the game of life. This was something I had to do once you were given intelligence, for the intellect demands fresh challenges in order to grow, and what is "fresh" outside the context of time?

[Please do not confuse intelligence with wisdom.]

Anyway, one of the darndest things about time is that it has a beginning, a middle, and an end. All of you boomers are somewhere in the middle, and maybe on the downside of middle at that, so it's a proper time to reflect a little on where you've been and where you're going. I know that sometimes this makes you a little sad, and this upsets Me.

But this fellow, Mark what's-his-name, doesn't seem to have the sense to be unduly concerned about this aging situation, so I figured I'd plug his act of lunacy in the hope that a little of his dementia will rub off on you. Besides, maybe if enough people buy his book, it'll go to his head and he'll stop bugging Me for a while.

I know, I need the rest.

MANOPAUSE

Part One

Smoke and Mirrors

1.

Shapes and Sizes

Physicists say the universe is proceeding to disorganization, an observation I can verify from my own personal experience. If memory still served me, which it rarely does anymore, I could refer to this axiom by its proper sobriquet. I think it's one of the laws of thermodynamics, although I see nothing either hot or dynamic about it.

(But I digress, which, I suppose, is yet another manifestation of the process of disorganization.)

I don't know exactly when it was that I went from long and lean to kind of short and dumpy; the segue from elegant to elephant is smooth indeed. The guy in the photograph, like the form in the mirror *before* activation of the suck-it-in reflex, seems a stranger, a middle-aged imposter who has stolen my name. I am powerless to stop the hoax, notwithstanding the sit-ups, the push-ups, the Rogaine, and yes, the suck-it-in reflex, because it is again, I suspect, a manifestation of this immutable law of thermodynamics.

Who could have foreseen the relevance of this when our high school physics teacher, Mr. Phlegma (now why the hell do I remember *that*?), struggled to keep us awake throughout its introduction? I don't see how *he* could have, because a recent resurfacing of my *Class of '63*

3

Taking off the edges.....

Twenty

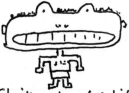

Triangles with tawny
steel cable connectors.

Thirty-five

Thick cubes of solid mass
No connectors needed.

Fifty

Nice, soft and cuddly
round balls of fluff and stuff.

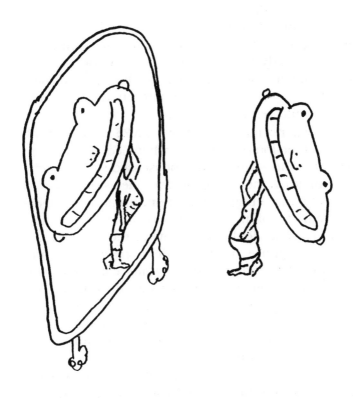

Mirror, mirror, on the wall.....
Suck it in, or it will fall.

yearbook revealed the "old fart" to have been perhaps ten years younger than I am now.

Anyway, I think long and lean becomes short and dumpy as a sort of resignation to the force of gravity, although why gravity doesn't proceed to disorganization instead of my body I don't know. The only person this seems to happen for is Michael Jordan, so maybe I should shave my head, save money on Rogaine, and everything would return to normal.

But what *is* normal for fifty, anyway? I seem to recall (and it wasn't too long ago, either) when people who were fifty were *old*, and—unless they possessed some genetic mutation making them eligible for television roles of kindly, understanding and non-threatening people—pretty bad-looking. What worries me is that now some fifty-year-old's look *regular*, while most other folks look *young*. I suppose this is a matter of perspective, and explains how it is that two orangutans can look good enough to each other to make them want to mate. Perspective is good if you're an orangutan, but I'm not so certain what it accomplishes for higher primates. Then again, what with late night television, I'm not sure who's the higher primate, either.

My kids (the boys, anyway) are at the age now when they dedicate a good bit of time to shaping their bodies. They are obsessed with adding bulk, and strut around puffing their necks for photographs as in a strange avian courtship ritual (even as I suck my stomach in for the same photo). Should I tell them now that everything they work so hard to put on upstairs will tumble downward in the blink of an eye? I think not; it's good they have their day in the sun.

The other thing I notice lately is that people seem to be getting larger and wider bodies, just like airplanes.

Yesterday I was in the airport building (I refuse to call it *terminal*) engaging in some idle people-watching, which is another sign of growing older, and there were a lot of middle-aged individuals who could scarcely qualify for the term anymore. I mean, there are entire blimps walking around in single pairs of shoes out there. Why is it that this happens?

The answer undoubtedly has to do with *metabolism*, the other dreaded enemy of those approaching fifty. Together with gravity, metabolism conspires to make every older person look, in a word, ridiculous. Here's how it works:

It takes a certain amount of energy to run our bodies, even if it doesn't seem like we're doing much. Just breathing, walking, and trying to figure out how to look lively burns calories, which is called your basal metabolic rate. (Notice how "metabolic" sounds like "diabolical.") When you're young, it takes about the same number of calories to run your body as you eat, so everything is okay. Experts tells us that this daily number of calories is about twenty-five hundred.

One day you wake up and, although you feel the same as you did yesterday, your brain has decided (overnight) to turn the switch that runs your metabolism to "off." It now requires approximately seven calories per day to run your body, which is the amount of energy released by digesting two bacteria. ANYTHING ELSE GOES DIRECTLY TO YOUR STOMACH AND SITS, quivering in the fear that you will discover it hiding there. The funny thing is, you *don't* notice it hiding there until somebody takes your picture without your realizing it, and then has the indecency to show it to you.

I recently read an article that pointed out the survival advantage of being able to store fat around the middle. It seems that in the real old days, before agriculture and the domestication of animals and rap groups (see THE ARTS, below), man didn't know where his next meal was coming from. (It sure as hell wasn't coming from women, who were already going through their Paleolithic Mesozoic Stratum [PMS] period.) So he gorged himself whenever there was food around, which encouraged the development of the first food storage device, the fat cell. This was such a big hit evolution-wise that in no time, people were sporting millions of fat cells.

I fantasize how Mother Nature experimented with where to put these fat cells, on men (naturally). Those sub-groups with fat cells on their noses suffocated and became extinct. Others with fat cells on a part of their anatomy too delicate to mention were initially the envy of the community, but died out the day the first sabre-toothed tiger chased down lunch. Those with fat around the middle were able to simply roll away from danger, living to see another day and eventually establishing the human race as we know it.

But enough of history. The fact is, I am resigned to fighting the battle of the bulge for the rest of my life: the sabre-toothed tiger has been replaced by the exercise guy who's always on TV in sports bars, who seems content to pass his days endlessly smiling and bouncing energetically in an attempt to convert his brain to mush before it can turn *his* metabolism switch to "off." It's too late for me. . . . I can feel his hot breath on the back of my neck, and he is gaining.

2.

The Vision Thing

One night, while I was blissfully asleep, my brain decided it no longer wanted to discern anything within four feet of itself, so it turned off the "near focus" switch. (This is located very close to the metabolism switch, and the two are frequently flicked off at the same time. After all, we wouldn't want to burn any unnecessary calories doing two things when one action will suffice, would we?)

The next day, everybody decided to print everything this big and since my arms are less than four feet long, I couldn't focus on anything.

Many people regard this as an incredible inconvenience, but I think it's proof of a benevolent God, Who probably never meant for us to read, anyway. (Why bother to read about anything if you could actually *do* it all, including dunk a basketball, in the Garden of Eden?)

I can think of several benefits that are conferred by this sudden farsightedness:

1. The hairs that begin growing out of your nose at about this time don't distract;
2. You can tell your wife that she still hasn't developed wrinkles and be honest about it;
3. Your reading speed improves as you find your-

self able to skim things (title pages, chapter headings, anything in bold font);

4. Reading glasses perched on top of the head keep thinning hair from blowing all around and making you appear even more befuddled than you actually are; and

5. If your hair's not thinning, you can hang reading glasses around your neck on something called a leash, leaving them to hang down and block the depressing view of your protruding gut.

(Please note: I have omitted referring to anything good that could come from positioning reading glasses on the third optional location, the tip of the nose. This is because nothing good *can* result from this bizarre behavior, unless one has a secret desire to look like every laughable and totally irrelevant character in the history of children's books.)

Another thing that happens when the "near focus" switch is turned off is that in order to actually read anything, your eyes require illumination levels previously achieved only by above-ground nuclear testing. I remember when my father-in-law would go around quietly turning on lamps everywhere I would sit to read; I began calling him "the old lamp lighter," and I'd smile in benevolent tolerance, muttering "Thank you" while wondering what on earth could have caused this fetish of his. I now realize he was thinking, "Just wait, in about seven minutes you won't be able to see squat," but he was too polite and too caring to say anything. I wish I could tell him I understand, but he's now in a place where he can see everything a hell of a lot better than I can, anyway.

3.

Time and Attitude

Once again, the physicist returns to haunt me. Einstein taught that time is relative, referring to how its passage changes with the speed of the observer. I am no Einstein, but I could have told him that the relationship certainly is an inverse one, because the more I slow down, the more time speeds up.

I used to wonder why it was that older people constantly underestimated the timing of past events; I now understand that things seem like they happened "just yesterday" because time passes so quickly as one ages. Writing this, it seems impossible that the United States Olympic hockey team triumphed over sixteen years ago.

The acceleration of the passage of time is so rapid that it has to be a reflection of more than just a simple relationship to the amount of time one has lived. I wonder if my internal clock is geared to the accrual of new experience, and after a while my having "been there, done that" makes noteworthy events more rare; time cannot be passing if my experiential clock isn't ticking, until someone asks if I recall this or that, and I may . . . but didn't that happen "just yesterday"?

The unfortunate corollary of this is that it creates the sensation that I am now hurtling through time, and since I am fifty, this is not particularly great news; the impres-

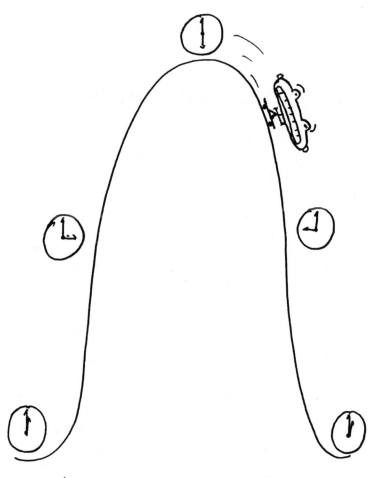

The skateboard ramp of life

sion is that I am on the other side of the hump, and the best of what's happened is behind me. All that awaits is system failure, and a seemingly accelerating one at that.

I personally don't believe this. There is a certain elegance to aging, or at least the opportunity for elegance that I find comfortable. It's not a simple willingness to pass the baton, although I am making progress in that direction; there is also an acquisition of perspective, a sweet appreciation for the passage of things. I take a strange comfort from this, that despite the insanity of a world gone amuck with self-serving rudeness, robins still fly north in the spring. Even Stokely Carmichael gets old, and his edges have rounded off a bit (though I think he's probably changed his name).

I also find myself playing the arithmetic game. . . . *I remember when we met, that was thirty-one years ago, in thirty-one years we'll be eighty-one . . . fifty, that's sixty-two percent of eighty, so I've got thirty-eight percent left, if I'm lucky. . . .* But I've found that while this can depress the hell out of me if I just sit thinking about it, it's a great motivator, too. Religious convictions aside, I'd like to leave a mark behind after all this, and it's difficult to justify watching *Cheers* with that clock ticking in the background, when the only mark I've made today is the depression in the couch. I can see it when I get up for a beer.

4.

You Gotta Have Heart

The heart occupies a very central place in the human situation. The Greeks attributed higher thought to this important organ, which explains why they abandoned physiology for the restaurant trade, and many societies believed the heart responsible for feelings and emotions. We still refer to virtue from grit to empathy as "heart."

This essay, though, will explore the heart for its most romantic property of all: *the heart as a pump.*

There is this thing in my chest, a little left of center, roughly the size of a kitten, upon which the continuation of my life is utterly and completely dependant. (I say "kitten" because we always hear that the heart is the size of one's fist. I dislike this analogy because of all the imagery the word "fist" brings to mind: aggression, struggle, intractability. I like to think of my heart as purring contentedly, completely satisfied, chugging along at a pace that can be maintained forever, without the sturm and drang of the "fist" thing.)

The constant if subconscious awareness of this makes me wary, because, after all, I've never even met this organ. I've never seen my heart, never heard it respond to anything I've ever told it or asked of it. As far as I can tell, it has a mind of its own, or, God forbid the Greeks were wrong, no mind whatsoever.

Think of it (I'm sure you have): there's this ball of muscle, all right, I'll say it, the size of a *fist*, about a foot and a half below my eyes, that has gone

boom-boom

some one-and-a-half billion times already, and I need it to keep doing that maybe what, another billion times or so. It might decide to do this, but then again, it might not. It may just say, "What the hell, I'm tired of doing the same stupid thing, day in, day out, lub-dub 'til it drives me crazy. All I look at are these four chambers, and all I get in return is a lot of pizza with mozzarella cheese that winds up on the walls of my arteries, as if my job weren't tough enough already and the big bastard I work for just keeps the pies coming, and I hear from the stomach they've just about had it with the pepperoni thing."

It has me concerned.

So I do to my heart what the experts tell me I need to do: push it 'til it's beating as fast as it can. I can't understand why something, which if left on its own will run at, say, sixty beats a minute, needs to be red-lined at about one-fifty for "sustained periods" of aerobic mad-ness *for its own good*. I picture that commercial where a little car engine (probably the size of a fist) is whining higher and higher in response to some asshole's lead foot, someone who must have the sensitivity of a heavy metal rocker because he can't hear that this little engine is about four milliseconds from completely exploding. The ad ends with the sound of a great sputtering, and I grab my chest in horror. In a moment I am patting my breast, assuring the precious motor beneath that I would never treat it this way, until I am interrupted by a pal's telephone call reminding me it's time to go work out.

17

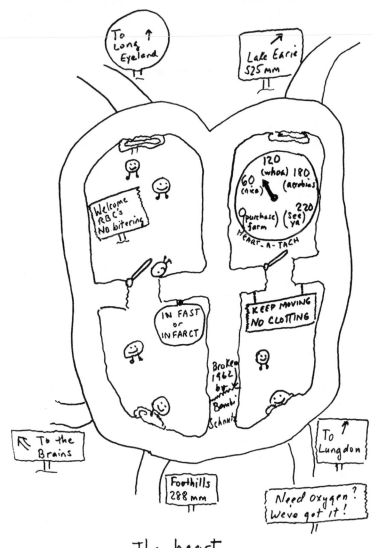

The heart

Every now and then, I am rudely made aware of my friend, the heart, when a twinge of *something* goes off somewhere "in there." Immediately I note whether it's from the left (bad) or right (okay, I think) side, whether it radiates down my left arm (very bad; this has never happened), or whether it's in my right arm (okay; tennis, golf, batting cages, still trying to pitch). Any day now I expect another organ system to catch the scent of rebellion: just to be safe, I skip the pepperoni.

5.

PC

Nothing strikes fear in my heart like these two seemingly-innocent letters of the alphabet. In the contemporary vernacular, they stand for two impossible-to-fathom concepts from hell, each as far away from my ability to comprehend as any mystery of the universe. The first thing I'm talking about, of course, is the:

Personal Computer

I'm still haunted by childhood dreams of finding myself in a class I've never been to before, a scant few moments before the final exam. I wake to find that reality is not much better.

I don't know how it happened that I was standing on the platform when the train pulled out, loaded with passengers bound for the glory of computer literacy, but suddenly everyone from pipsqueaks to grandmothers is "surfing the net," whatever the hell that means. I think it refers to the fact that all kinds of stuff is available from one computer system to another, *over the telephone*, and computers now have the ability to call one another and chat a while.

Imagine such a conversation: "Hiya, Aptiva, this is Tandy. I couldn't help noticing your hard drive. Whatya say we hook our modems together and fax awhile?" No wonder Congress wants to investigate this stuff.

The strange thing is, humans seem to enjoy this voyeuristic form of communication. I can't for the life of me figure this out; I understand that we've developed a nifty-quick way to share information, but as far as I can tell, nothing's been done to improve the quality of the information itself. (This is similar to recent improvements in television technology, where it is now possible to discern individual specs of flea guano on the contemporary screen. Unfortunately, this is also the intellectual level of current programming.)

I don't know about you, but I wouldn't spend three bucks to listen to some idiot who's dumb enough to have spent three grand on a machine so he can tell me, a perfect stranger, what he thinks. In fact, if his investment strategy is any indication of his sense of judgment, I'd pay three bucks *not* to listen to anything he might want to share with me.

Yet I'm willing to acknowledge that I'm missing something here. After all, just because computers are embraced in a society where the majority of its citizens don't know what a molecule is, doesn't mean it's dumb to go out and buy one just because everyone else has. I'm probably just jealous because I slept through the class.

The other contemporary reference to "PC," political correctness, is the great buzzword of our enlightened societal super-ego. I'm not sure what it means, but it seems that a corollary of this doctrine is: **DON'T OFFEND ANYONE**. Just about everyone I know (outside of New York City) wouldn't argue with this basic premise, but what I can't seem to master is the incredible lengths of behavior modification one is supposed to go through

21

PC's from hell

just to avoid the *remote possibility* that anyone in the solar system could have been, might be, or perhaps will in the future be put out by anything I might do, say or think. As the Buddhist monk spends a lifetime looking down lest he inadvertently squash a bug with his feet, so we are to examine the content of our actions prior to doing them, lest we dash someone's feelings on the pavement of life. The irony is, it seems to me, that those of whose sensibilities we are to be most respectful are defended by the most rude and crass lunatic fringe this society is capable of spawning.

I'm sorry if I sound a little vitriolic, but then, I'm fifty and supposed to sound that way. Be careful: don't say anything to hurt my feelings, or I'll smack you right in the face.

6.

Oxymoron I: Sports at Fifty

One of the cruel jokes of aging is that while you can't remember where you just parked the car an hour ago, the mind recalls with infinite sweetness just how it felt some thirty years past to make that lightning-quick cut, leaving the defensive back looking for his jock. Or the whip of the arm as the ball flew as though shot out of a cannon, getting across the diamond in complete defiance of gravity.

I also remember exactly when it was that the reality of my declining flexibility hit me—smack between the eyes. It was a few years ago, when my son and I were playing "long toss" with a hardball prior to his warming up to pitch. Chip was a professional at the time, a twenty-three-year-old strapping young lad, a six-foot-five windmill built to throw; I was suffering under the delusion that I could still cut the mustard, a misimpression that was to last another few minutes as he backed up farther and farther between tosses. Soon the unthinkable happened: I threw the ball back and it bounced before it reached him.

Certain that I must have lost my footing, or something, I waited impatiently for the return throw so I could reassure myself with a frozen rope. Looking back, there was a momentary pause in his transition from catch to throw, and it should have told me something. He had seen it, too, and I think he wanted to believe I'd slipped even more than I wanted to. But we both knew better.

I'll skip the rest of the details, but it was pretty gory. My arm, no, not just the arm, but my legs and torso felt *different*, like a unit with no joints or levers.

I've since learned to accommodate, and even utilize my newfound stiffness. The golf ball still flies pretty far despite a radical shortening of the backswing, and no wonder: the whole body resists coiling like an intractable garden hose, so that tension roughly equivalent to the force required for atom-smashing is generated just by taking the club back to shoulder level.

All of a sudden, doubles tennis seems like a real sport, and I find myself committing more thought (if not actual time) to that great misadventure of the non-athlete: **working out**.

Working out is the modern term for exercise, and I think it's interesting to note that the action word for sports is **play**, while that for exercise is **work**. Never has a semantic distinction been more right on. I've heard people say they *like* working out (which, of course, if true, would constitute prima facie evidence for commitment on the grounds of certifiable insanity), but I think in most cases this is simply an observation of the overheated brain. True, it does feel better after you work out, but the same may be said of hitting one's head repeatedly with a hammer: it sure feels great when you stop. I find the pleasure of each roughly equivalent, except that the latter will land you in an asylum, whereas the former may bag you your own daytime program on ESPN (albeit right after the International Poultry Plucking time trials).

I am not referring here to training regimens that are designed to enhance performance in a particular endeavor of athletics, but rather to programs that purport to *shape a new you* with a modest investment of perhaps ten or twenty minutes every other day, and with an additional small investment for video tapes, rocking devices right out of the Marquis de Sade catalogue, mantras, timers, balms, liquids, dietary items, absurd-looking tight stretchy things made of materials having no vowels, running shoes, walking shoes, workout shoes, cross-training shoes, and unmentionable undergarments that are for some perverse reason worn on the outside. I must admit, though, that these programs do reshape; in no time they'll take inches off your rear (assuming that's where you keep your wallet).

Eventually, people find when they reach fifty or so that working out just isn't working out, so they put all their stuff in a big closet (usually belonging to one of the kids away at college) and reinvest in new accoutrements so they can begin walking. Not regular walking, but a bizarre form of ambulation that can only be visually described as, well, quintessentially stupid-looking. You know the walk I mean: shorts or sweat pants (really shiny), pretty high socks, walking shoes, flappy top, some not-quite-discernible electronic gadget about the neck with wires going to or coming from various segments of the anatomy, dumbbells or some kind of weights in the hands, and (here comes the real dorky part) *the person is swinging his arms back and forth in a maniacal attempt to fly, begin cartwheeling*, or something else nature hadn't intended for the human form.

Experts tell us that this regimen, although strange-looking, will add years to one's lifespan. I don't think it's an even trade.

One benefit to aging is that even as your skills begin to fade, there is the pleasure of working with the kids and

The modern workout aficionado

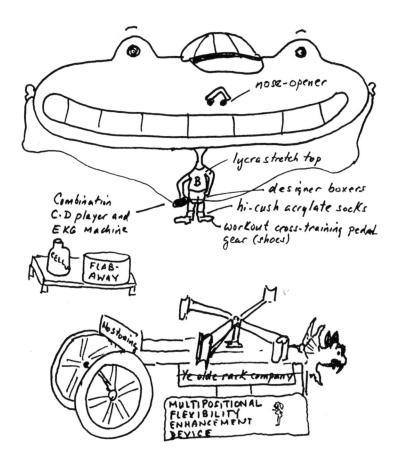

nose-opener

lycra stretch top

designer boxers

hi-cush acrylate socks

Combination C.D player and EKG Machine

workout cross-training pedal gear (shoes)

CELL

FLAB-AWAY

Abstoning

Ye olde rack company

MULTIPOSITIONAL FLEXIBILITY ENHANCEMENT DEVICE

watching them grow in stature and physical accomplishment. The transition from athlete to athletic supporter happens automatically (though insidiously) when you have kids who play sports. Reveling in their accomplishments is the perfect balm for a diminution of your own, and somehow it seems that this is as it should be. I had always thought it would be hard not to experience a sense of loss while watching kids shine, but I have to admit it's better than any glow I may have felt from my own accomplishment.

7.

I Remember When . . .

Wistful reminiscing is a practice in which we all indulge with increasing frequency and longing as we get older. One would think this tendency would ebb somewhat as the aging process takes its toll on the memory, but our powers of recollection seem to fade according to modern accounting principles: Last In, First Out. Unfortunately, this makes us less relevant (or at least less topical) as time goes on.

Nostalgia is so common in older folks (and always has been) that one of two explanations exists for its universality: either things have been getting worse for centuries and will probably continue to get worse, or there is a universal distrust for change, making it difficult for us to objectively evaluate things new. I'm certain it's the latter, because in many areas the present is a lot better than the past (hygiene, medicine, and environmental awareness, to name a few). Yet, most of us would agree that progress comes with a price, and who is not disturbed by what sure as hell seems to be a degradation of the human spirit in today's "gimme" jungle?

Surprisingly, I've noticed this tendency in the kids, too. Their favorites are war stories from the ancient past of their childhood, partly because these tales of infamy usually relate to calamities that were funny to begin with, and on which time has played its trick of smoothing out the bumps and heightening the humor. Nostalgia is not an exclusive practice of the older generation: I've recently heard twenty-year-old's go on with one another over the comparative lameness of contemporary Saturday morning cartoons.

Another manifestation of increasing years is the tendency to repeat oneself. Again, last in, first out, so sometimes the rate of repetition is embarrassingly high. Eventually you become so defensive about it that you skip entire stories, thinking, *Now did I say that already? I don't want to appear really out of it, so maybe I'd better not say anything.*

Another manifestation of aging is the tendency to say things over and over again.

Still, it's fun to recall events of the past, and many times it's the recollective act itself that is so enjoyable rather than the merits or import of the thing recalled. The enormous popularity of trivia games is an example, and it is often the most inane jingle that brings the biggest kneeslap.

In this spirit, I offer you fifty-year-old's the following list of memory-tweakers:

My fellow Americans . . . B-o, n-o, m-o, oh-oh-oh, it's Bonomo's—candy (what ever happened to Turkish Taffy?). . . . There's a long drive, to deep center field, it's go-ing, go-ing, gone! . . . That's one giant leap for mankind. . . . I can't get no . . . Plunk your magic twanger, Froggy. . . . I am not a crook. . . . N-E-S-T-L-E-S, Nestles makes the very best . . . Duck, and cover! . . . Hold the chicken salad? . . . It's called Sputnik. . . . We're bigger than Jesus. . . . I have decided not to run. . . . Dance with me, Henry. . . . Godzilla versus Rodan. . . . My Lai. . . . Ask not what your country can do . . .

We will bury you. . . . Tomorrow your hair will be sunshine bright. . . . There she is. . . . I wanna hold your hand. . . . Don't just feed me bananas. . . . Able to leap tall buildings . . . The kick is up, it's good!

8.

Politics

They say that we become jaded in some areas of life as we get older; in no endeavor is this more apparent than politics. I guess you can be fed just so much bullshit before you realize, "Say, this tastes just like bullshit!"

Unfortunately, because the infamy of those who serve themselves at the expense of the public interest is so aggrandized by the press, we tend to look at all politicians with the same degree of disgust. There are actually those who dedicate their careers to serving their country, although none of those good people are from *this* country.

Since we've had such difficulty lately finding capable people to represent us in government, it might not be a bad idea to reexamine the criteria used to measure their qualifications. Maybe if we were more realistic about our expectations, the performance of those in office would come closer to matching them. After all, one of the obligations of society's elders is to confer the benefits of their experience to the young, so that the newer generation doesn't have to repeat their mistakes. (Except that younger generations never listen to older generations, unless they're from the African veldt or something, where, ironically, societies never seem to change. But forget about that for the moment.)

In this spirit of bestowing tribal wisdom, then, I offer the following quiz for those who would seek the public trust:

Candidate Screening Test
(Democrats: use the enclosed golf pencil;
Republicans: any Mont Blanc is acceptable)

1. How much money do you make a year?
a. under $100,000;
b. over $100,000
If you answered "a," above, go to question 2 (skip #3); if you answered "b," above, go to question 3 (skip #2);

2. How much money will it take for you to satisfy your unrealized personal material needs before you can start to work on our stuff?
a. under a cool mil;
b. How many years can I stay?

3. Why do you suppose you have this Messiah complex?
a. I am very short;
b. I worry constantly about the welfare of others.
(Note: if you answered "b" to number 3, above, see a doctor immediately.)

Another good thing about a screening test like this is that we could have each person of age submit his or her own question, making the voter feel like he is more a part of the selection process. This would be a big improvement over the way it is now, when you sometimes may have to choose between a crook and an incompetent, which is more like deciding whether you want to be executed either by having your eyes gouged out or by listening to endless tapes of Jay Leno monologues. What kind of a choice is that? (Although if you ask me, I would pick the former.)

My personal question would be: Is either your first or last name that of an amphibian?

Now this may seem like a stupid question to you, but think about it a minute: here you are, the proud parent of a brand new baby, and something about it makes you want to name it "Toad" or "Mugwump" or "Newt." Either there was something you saw in the kid to inspire you this way, or there wasn't, meaning you are so perverted that you may not be capable of mastering the parenting skills of mammals (or at least higher reptiles). I don't want a kid raised like an amphibian telling *me* what to do.

Anyway, we'd best be organizing ourselves about this politics business, because experts tell us that we baby-boomers constitute the most significant voting bloc in the history of this country. This means we need to formulate our "agenda," which is a fancy official-sounding word meaning "things we think would be fair to do for us." (This is not to be confused with that other political term, "selfish interests," which is used to describe the wish-lists of *others*.)

In order to save you some time, I've already thought about what some of the things on this agenda might be:

1. Take all embarrassing advertisements relating to products that would serve previously-unfathomable but now dimly-recognizable plights of the human situation from television, radio, and print. No-no topics would include constipation, hearing loss, vision loss, sphincter loss (*any* sphincter; in fact, the term sphincter should not be used, ever, by anybody outside of a doctor's office),

hair loss, memory loss, denture loss, loss of consort, sexual dysfunction, and any product promoted by Ed McMahon.

2. I'm too depressed to go on. You do it.

9.

Out of It (and Loving It)

Do you remember the first time it hit you, that your parents were, well, not really *where it's at*? The realization that the generation above you is not only capable of error but is in fact doomed to a life of continuous blunder begins on Tuesday and is complete by Wednesday, and this only gets more apparent as the gap between you and your elders increases. Unfortunately, after a while something occurs that makes it impossible for you to continue to dismiss those *younger* than *you* as totally irrelevant. Usually this happens with your first speeding ticket handed to you by a police officer no older than twelve, or the realization that the Yankee first baseman whose career you've started following is the age of your son.

Congratulations! You've officially entered the land of the Out of It, that pasture to which you've been consigning parents and other irrelevants ever since you discovered that they thought Led Zeppelin was a blimp that couldn't fly. Suddenly a lot of what's happening around you doesn't make any sense; sure, sometimes this confuses you, but most of the time, things don't add up because the world has gone crazy.

I have decided that a lot of this inability to understand what the hell is going on with "the younger generation" is due to, yes, here it comes, a *failure to communicate* (sorry). So, in the interest of bridging the gap, I offer the following survey for the young to complete, so that they may be better understood by us who live in the Land of the Out-of-it:

Reach Out for Enlightenment

Please complete this enlightenment questionnaire, so that we, the aging, may better understand you, our youth, on whom we will increasingly rely in our yet more advanced years:

Part One: Girls Only

1. I think I look really neat in combat boots because:
2. I think I look really neat with tattoos because:
3. I think I look really trendy with my hair chopped off because:
4. I share my sisters' sense of gender assertion because:

Part Two: Boys Only

1. I like to kiss my girlfriend wearing paper clips through her lips because:
2. I like my girlfriend to dress in combat boots, wear tattoos, and chop her hair off because:
3. What is gender assertion?

Part Three: For All Others

1. I think putting big letters with little letters with no apparent system like in contemporary ads and ESPN-2 looks really cool because:
2. I'm not going to fill out any more stupid surveys, because I'm really pissed that you've handed us over a world where, for the first time in the history of this country, it's in worse shape than it was when *you* got it.
   Oops.

NinEty's dReAM GiRL

10.

I Heard the News Today—Oh, Boy

Americans are fascinated by the news. Other societies offer greetings with such expressions as "Hello" or "How are you?," while we ask, "What's new?," "What's up?," "What's happening?"

A huge industry has evolved to serve this preoccupation with knowing what's going on. Think of it: without our desire to find out the latest, there would be no need for newspapers, TV news or radio news. Can you imagine how many billions of dollars are used to fuel this enterprise?

This makes it all the more ironic that, in fact, there is no such thing as news. Yep, now that I've witnessed the comings and goings of the human race for some fifty years, I am here to report that nothing, that's right, nothing you will hear on the "news" tonight, tomorrow night, or almost any other night will strike you as new. When was the last time you turned to your fellow-sufferer as you struggled through the oh-so-serious intonation of the newscaster and remarked, "Gee, how interesting . . . that's something I never knew before!"?

It's an oxymoron that what passes for news is really old hat. Sure, the names in the stories change once in a while, but the stories themselves never do.

I can prove this: I recently came across a script right

out of the newsroom of a famous network. It is reproduced here in the complete security of knowing that they
will never come after me, because to do so would be
admitting its authenticity. You'll see what I mean.

Good (morning, afternoon, evening, God), everyone, I'm
(Peter, Tom, Connie, your waiter), and here is the news.
On the (international, national, local) scene, members of
the (PLO, SLA, MTV, ASPCA) told reporters that they will
no longer tolerate being (bombed, heckled, taunted,
sucked up to, treated as second-class citizens) by the
(Israelis, Imperial Wizard, opposite sex). Now, this. . . .

BREAK FOUR MINUTES FOR COMMERCIALS

Elsewhere, scientists report that the (Earth, planets,
Sun, ozone layer, manatee) is (not real, shrinking, spin-
ning, doomed, absurd, mating) even as we speak, and
there is (no hope, a good chance, a moon out tonight).
When we return, we'll have the latest from our Chanel No.
5 Accu-Righton-Exacto-Weather. Now, this. . . .

BREAK SIX MINUTES FOR COMMERCIALS

Hi, I'm (Marty, Doreen, Spin), and here's the latest
from our Accu-Weather radar. Notice this band of (show-
ers, tornados, Indians, angels) moving in our direction
counterclockwise around this (low, high), which may pick
up (moisture, dry air) from the (ocean, Sahara), in which
case it may very well (rain, snow, stay dry); otherwise, it
won't. So tomorrow's forecast is for (continued) (precipi-
tation, drought), and I'd say the chances for this are about
50 percent, give or take a half. Coming up next, sports,
but now, this. . . .

BREAK TWO MINUTES FOR COMMERCIALS

We will return in a moment.

BREAK THREE MINUTES FOR COMMERCIALS

Hiya, I'm your virile local market ex-jock, (first name), and here's the latest from the world of sports. From the gridiron, (name) shocked the sports world today when (he, she) held out for (pick an absurd number) million dollars in order to begin (playing, thinking about signing, cheering, therapy) for the (team). On the diamond, free agent (name) says he won't re-sign for his old team, citing bad feelings over their failure to hand over all money from operations. Finally, basketball star (name), tired of being treated like an object, says he is quitting hoops for (a year, knitting, nuclear physics).

That's it for tonight. For the entire Chanel No. 5 news team, I'm (who cares?). . . . Good (day, night, riddance).

Admit it . . . sound familiar? You stay up for *this*? Imagine, the very last thing you hear before going to bed (perchance, to dream) or the very first thing you wake up to is a measured dose of poison, administered with a carefully calculated mind-numbing slew of commercials so you won't even realize that they're killing your spirit. Who would want to support a species that was defined by the "news"? No wonder we're out there killing each other . . . everyone else is doing it, and besides, we're just scum because (Dan, Tom, Ken-doll) says so. And you believe him, don't you?

11.

The Arts at Fifty

Art is an expression of its time, which explains why people generally become less apt to understand contemporary art as their stewardship of the popular culture passes on to subsequent generations. Boomers approaching fifty are now once removed from the current young "movers and shakers" generation, whose own kids are entering the world even as we speak. This means that in ten years, our *grandchildren* will begin selecting the sounds that shape the music charts.

I find this pretty unsettling, since I'm unable to fathom much of what passes for entertainment *right now*. I know that I am not alone: the other day on the bus I overheard a group of young teens referring to the whapping noise blasting from their stereo as "post regressive rap" and "fusion synthesis," and in a little while, the lady seated next to me tried to get off the bus when they turned the boombox off. She had thought the engine died.

This confusion is not confined to the auditory arts. I was watching a highly-acclaimed movie the other day (*that* should have warned me right away), when I realized that the scene I had just witnessed had not happened yet, and the one I was currently watching happened before (a sort of "flashback to the future," as the eight-year-old kid seated next to me pointed out to his buddy). I had no clue what the hell was going on, but I was beginning to understand why the critics were calling the screenwriter "brilliant"; you had to be in order to figure out the sequence, let alone content, of what was on the screen. My head ached for days after that.

You can get a good idea of contemporary attitudes as they are conveyed through the art and style of advertisements, especially photo ads that promote things to the young and/or upwardly mobile. One thing worries me: have you noticed how people in magazines and on billboards don't smile any more? They tend to look vaguely pissed off, or just plain vague or "gommy." Maybe it's me, but I get the impression the director is telling the model, don't ingratiate yourself to the audience with a smile, just ignore them and look bored or something. Also, the models are missing one or several pieces of clothing in a lot of these ads, frequently inappropriately, and many of the pictures are in black and white. The lettering in the text of the ad is uneven, with different fonts and lower case and capital letters arranged in no particular order.

I think most people my age look at this stuff and say, "I don't understand this, so it must be art, and it's probably good art because it's in black and white and the people in the ads are either serious or dorky-looking." But it just may be that it's a bunch of crap; or it may be that you have to be young to understand it, it's an attitude thing, and while we're used to having companies say, "Please buy our stuff," the current attitude is, "Here's our stuff, we don't give a rat's ass about you or whether you buy our stuff or not, but here it is anyway." Maybe it's reverse psychology . . . ooh, wow, these jeans guys are so cool, way cooler than *me*, and so maybe I can be cool and aloof too and not give a rat's ass about things either if I can only buy a pair of these jeans . . . .

Have you noticed how the field of legitimate art (painting, sculpture, that kind of stuff) has no particular style or signature right now? All the "creative" energy is being funneled into commercial art or cinematographic art (that's ads and movies if you're over fifty), probably because it pays so well, and it's readily available to huge segments of the public. This is very fortunate, because it enables me to present the following *condensed guide to art* as embodied in those two sacred media forms, whereas even *I* wouldn't have the nerve to pass myself off as possessing any kind of ability to appreciate the more subtle forms of art, such as sculpture, oils, and tractor-pulling.

Here it is:

The Handy Guide to Art and Style

PART ONE: The Ads

a. When looking at an advertisement, especially ones in print, note first whether or not it is in color. If it is, the product can't be that stylish, because every toad knows that real artsy stuff is always in black and white, and if you even begin to doubt this, check out the prices for developing black and white film compared to color film. *They* know.

b. Okay, assuming the ad is in black and white, how do you know whether the stuff in the ad is right for *you*, even if it is artsy? If you're female, you don't need to read this part, because you're born with a genetic program telling you the right answer about these things (it's located on the same chromosome that enables you to fold clothing faster than the male eye is capable of following). If you're

Old Ad

♪ Please buy, won't you try
Yucco toothpaste, it's
♫ the greatest for you!
Yay! Whoopie!

Modern Ad

GET BEnT, InsiGnificaNt
SLiMe. Yucco TooThPaStE.
IF you'RE LUCKY.
— It's ReAL —

male, and coming on fifty, you have no *concept* whether the product, be it something to drink, wear, sniff, look at, eat, ogle, medicate with, make love with, or improve your personal hygiene, will make you a more acceptable member of society. For this, you'll have to ask a woman, but don't worry: even if you don't ask, she'll *tell you.*

PART TWO: The Movies

a. Before settling in to critique a contemporary movie, you must first be able to classify it. Here are a few pointers on how to do this based on a very few clues:

1. FOREIGN FILM: CREDITS: Names with umlauts, breathy la-la female singing in background, black-and-white, lint flecks in background of film; OPENING SCENE: contains a bicycle, cars with indistinguishable backs and fronts, actress with an indistinguishable back and front with very short hair and at least one bare breast, fornicating or cooking but always looking bored; MAIN PART: male lead with concave chest and hair a lot longer than female, muttering and threatening to blow something up; CLIMAX: nothing happens.

CRITIQUE SUGGESTION: Critics always rate foreign films highly, because they are gloomy people who are always pissed off that they aren't good enough to actually *do* anything themselves. But you should rate them highly, too, because how the hell are you going to figure out a European film on your own?

2. AMERICAN FILM, ADVENTURE/ACTION TYPE: OPENING CREDITS: car drives up on curb, blows up from impact; OPENING SCENE: Strange-looking person blows up lots of people and buildings, then melts into mercury; MAIN PART: Strange-looking person shoots

46

everything on the planet, vows to return (but to what?); CLIMAX: what, are you kidding? There is no climax in films like these: it takes three seconds to crank up to full bore, and stays there 'til it's over.

CRITIQUE SUGGESTION: You don't need to critique this type of movie; no one does. They are simply shells designed to show off pyrotechnics and special visual effects.

3. AMERICAN FILM, RELATIONSHIPS TYPE: OPENING CREDITS: background music has a lot of violins, maybe an oboe, and is very sweet. Colors are kind of pastel-ish. This is your clue that you've been roped into seeing a "relationships" movie, probably by a female, where nothing happens during the entire film except different women laugh and cry a lot, together, while one or more menfolk bumble and bungle through the background. YOU DON'T NEED TO CRITIQUE THIS KIND OF MOVIE; no woman would pay any attention to your opinion of it, anyway, and you wouldn't want to admit to any man that you'd seen it.

4. AMERICAN MOVIE, HOT: OPENING CREDITS: who remembers?; OPENING SCENE: Boy meets girl, initially both shy, soon wind up grappling in bed, boy screws girl (right there on the screen), boy introduces himself to girl; MAIN PART: boy meets new girl, screws her, original girl accuses him of having no values, she gets very cozy with second girl (do people really do this stuff?); CLIMAX: yes, often.

CRITIQUE SUGGESTION: you may wing this one, but use some of the -otic words (erotic, exotic, neurotic, quixotic), and, if the movie seemed pretty fancy filming-wise, you may want to use some -esque words, too (Kafka-esque is a big one, although no one, including Franz, knows what this means).

We hope you find this guide helpful in assisting your belated and ultimately futile attempt to reunite with the "in" crowd.

12.

A Day in the Life at Command Central

Great strides have been made over our lifetime in the field of medicine, where the dramatic life-or-death struggle for Medicare dollars goes on every day. Tools that weren't even in the imagination when we were kids are standard weapons in the arsenal of the modern doctor, things like endoscopes that enable the practitioner to see all the way to the bottom of the rectum (*from your mouth*) and high-deductible insurance cards that enable his nurse to see all the way down to the bottom of your wallet.

I was recently asked to volunteer my body to test a very new device that *actually enables doctors to listen to the brain working.* I don't mean an EEG where all you get are little squiggly lines across a chart (which, come to think of it, is probably a fair representation of what usually goes through my head), but a wonderful gadget that picks up your brain waves and translates them into actual text, producing a record of the body's actions as dictated by the brain. I have reproduced this transcript here because it offers interesting insight into how the male mind copes with the stresses of daily living, especially from the perspective of a body that is becoming a little unfamiliar with itself as it ages.

One end of this device is passed into the Command

Center of the brain; the other end sticks out your nose and broadcasts a signal through the air to a computer with a software program that translates brain activity into language. It then types out what's going on. Pretty nifty, eh?

I wore the device for the better part of a day, beginning at midnight. Here are some excerpts:

4:37 A.M.

Sir, we are picking up a strong signal from the lower abdominal area. I think it's Mr. Bladder. Should I. . . .

Hell, that's the third time this week. Why can't he just hold his water, like he used to?

Uh, sir, we are getting a substantial pressure build-up in the lower abdomen, and Mr. Rectum is threatening to. . . .

All right, goddamn it, the boss ain't gonna like it . . . alert the reticular activating system. We've got to wake up the poor SOB.

Aye-aye, sir.

ATTENTION, ATTENTION. YOU MUST WAKE UP. YOUR BLADDER PRESSURE IS APPROACHING THAT OF MOUNT SAINT HELENS. YOU MUST, REPEAT, MUST GET UP.

I'm not getting a response, sir. Uh-oh . . .

What's that?

Sphincter alarm, sir. I think . . . oh, no, he's dreaming he's in the bathroom again.

Sound the alarm! Emergency awakening procedures. He's gonna wet the bed, for God's sake.

Should we . . . ?

Yes! Play Engelbert Humperdinck's greatest hits on full volume. . . . He'll wake up screaming, but at least we won't have to sleep in all that. . . .

6:14 A.M.

Sir, I hate to wake you, but. . . .

What is it now? What is it with you? For the last couple of years now, you call me at this ungodly hour, and the alarm hasn't even. . . .

Sir, I'm sorry, but he wants to get up. He's been lying here, fully awake, for ten minutes now, and the input board is registering full signal strength from Mr. Eyeball, Mr. Eardrum and, whoa, lookee here, even Mr. Pe– . . . Mr. Pe– . . . oh, God, how I hate that name. . . .

I thought you said he wanted to get up. Or did you mean . . . ?

7:04 A.M.

Aahh, for Crissake, get the short-term memory center on the line.

Uh, sir, he's on vacation again. . . .

What? He's always . . . never mind, try the scalp. The boss is in the shower, and he wants to know whether he's just washed his hair, or if he was starting to wash his hair. . . .

7:13 A.M.

Sir, it's Mr. Tummy again. He wants to know why he has to suck himself in all the time, whenever Mr. Eyeball looks at him.

7:53 A.M.

Goddamn it, when is that short-term memory coming back? The boss wants to know the name of that little boy. . . .

Sir, that's his son. I think we could consult the long-term memory for that one. . . .

51

8:01 A.M.

Sir, we are getting into another situation. Mr. Tummy is threatening to blow himself up if we don't stop eating this muffin.

Two bites! The poor SOB has had just two bites and a thimbleful of juice, and the old gasbag is bitching?

SIR! SIR! Pardon me for interrupting, but . . . yes, I think it's . . . it's faint, but I think Mr. Bowel is moving! This could be the magic moment we've all been waiting for! Shall I notify Mr. Rectum?

Nah . . . could be another false alarm. Wait and see.

Well, perhaps I should give Mr. Feet a call, just so he gets ready to motor. . . .

8:22 A.M.

Sir, it's Mr. Eyeball on the line. He is demanding that Mr. Arm go to maximum extension on the newspaper, or he claims we don't have a chance in hell of making out the box score. He's also requesting the entire Torso group rotate toward the light.

8:53 A.M.

All right, everybody . . . that's a wrap! The boss is in the office, so he won't be needing his brains 'til lunchtime. Everybody take five, go to full autonomic mode, activate vegetative functions, all higher thought processes shut down on my mark, five, four, three. . . .

11:52 A.M.

Sir, we're getting rumbling from Mr. Tummy, indicating the lunch hour is upon us.

Okay, power up the cortex; higher thought master switch to "enable."

Sir, we really must do something with that master switch; it gets harder to activate all the time lately. Ooops.

What's wrong?

Mr. Eyeball reports an image dead ahead. . . . It's Ms. Lollapalooza, that . . .

The babe? Lemme see the screen. What's she got on today?

It must be a doozie. I'm getting auto-release indicators from Mr. Adrenal. . . . There goes Mr. Heart. . . . Tachometer reading 120 and climbing fast, sir! Mr. Eyeball reports Ms. Lollapalooza is approaching. Sir! What'll we do?!

Activate emergency conversation center, pronto. Put all memory centers on scan, something interesting for God's sake, not another "Did you see 'Friends' last night?" bonehead opener . . . crap! Put Mr. Tummy on full contraction status and hold 'til further notice; put Mr. Lung on it, too.

Mayday! Mayday! Mr. Rectum reports enormous pressure buildup. . . . Oh, no, it's another gas leak! . . . I can't raise Mr. Sphincter!!!! . . . Oooooh, nooooo!! . . .

12:22 P.M.

Sir, Mr. Saliva is indicating in his normally embarrassing way that he would like us to go for the pepperoni. If Mr. Tummy finds out, he'll flip.

Tell Peepers to rotate left thirty degrees and take her down six inches. We've got to get the Boss to focus on the salad part of the menu.

1:06 P.M.

Okay, you guys, let's slow it down. Go into full nap

53

profile. Tell Mr. Eardrum he's got the watch; I think it's Lefty's turn.

4:22 P.M.

Sir, I think we'd better power up. Mr. Short-Term Memory dropped by to pick up his check, and reminded me that we've got the company softball game this evening.

Z-Z-Z-Zmpf!? Whazzat? Geez, we're not outta here for a half hour. . . . Why'dja wake me up so soon?

Sir, you may recall what happened the last time we didn't stretch out. You know how you hate the smell of hospitals. I suggest we follow the full warm-up drill they showed on the Jack LaLanne show the other. . . .

Are you pullin' my chain? That was for old. . . .

Yes, sir, I know. . . . It's difficult. We do have a hard time remembering our age, don't we?

Don't patronize me, you little shithead. I'm still two hundred pounds of male animal ready to pounce.

Of course you are, sir. Two-sixteen, in fact. Sir, may I give the order?

Go ahead, you wuss.

6:25 P.M.

I'm the best. . . . I couldda made it here in center, like the Mick . . . it's pretty far to the backstop from here, though. Tell Mr. Eyeball to give me a little more range on his focus; I can't see jack . . .

Sir!! Mr. Ear reports a sharp crack from the plate. I think it's coming this way!!

Eyeballs to emergency scan! Mr. Feet, full alert!

Sir, eyeballs have picked up the ball on a heading zero-one-niner. I make that deep left center.

Feet, take off! Activate eyeball input directly to cortical calculator, and go to full auto-pilot for intercept.

54

Sir! Cortical calculator extrapolates us four feet short of intercept, ball will arrive in six seconds!

Bullshit! This one's for the Mick . . . go to after-burners, legs on full aerobic and anaerobic combustion!

Sir! We can't! With the kind of shape we're in, something will blow for sure!

That's an order! Two-point-four seconds to intercept!

We're not gonna make it!

One-point-three . . . DIVE! WE CAN DO IT!! DIVE, GODDAMN IT!!

7:15 P.M.

Sir, it was nice of the whole team to stop by, wasn't it? Now, try not to notice the odor . . .

Goddamn, Mr. Groin. We coulda had it. Dontcha think?

Of course, sir. Next time, for sure.

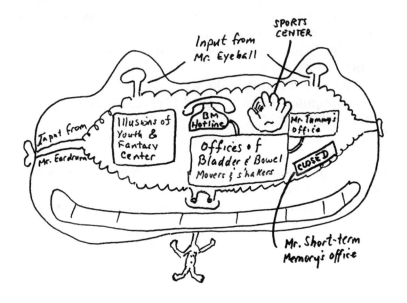

Command Central

Part Two

Getting Your Stuff Together (Straight from the Shoulder)

13.

The Trouble with Things Today . . .

I remember years ago hearing these words of introduction and immediately lapsing into a coma, managing to roll my eyes just before sinking into unconsciousness. Of course, the person saying it had to be a minimum of twice my age, and was probably about to blast me and everything about "the younger generation" to kingdom come.

Those of us who are now around fifty grew up in a time when life was a lot different than it is now, and much the same could be said of our own parents' heyday, comparing it with ours. I suspect it has always seemed this way, and that the morality d'jour is generally thought to be shot to hell by those who were raised in an earlier and more strict environment.

This doesn't mean that we can discount all changes; in fact, many of my contemporaries are convinced that we are going to hell in a handbasket. They feel there is something missing, something gone from the human spirit, and it frightens them. What worries me is that there may soon emerge a generation that doesn't *realize* something is missing, because then I think we could be in trouble. You can't fix a broken cyclotron if you don't know it was designed to smash atoms (you may not be able to fix it anyway; the instructions on those things are a real bear).

Our generation has been psychoanalyzed to death: the Kennedy assassination, Vietnam, Watergate: you know the litany. Disillusionment in and distrust for the establishment (what, *our* government screw with *us*?), the poor disenfranchised kids who grew up hating authority only to find we had *become* the authority. Baby boomers who, having rejected the values of their parents, became parents themselves and then didn't really know what values to teach their own kids.

So we experimented. Don't parent from an authoritarian point of view; explain things, reason with your child, be honest with everyone's emotions, be real, be true to yourself, leave if the relationship's not working (kids can tell if you're faking it anyway), everybody's doing it, even if it doesn't feel quite right deep inside in that place you keep trying to cover up; commitments are fine, but the highest commitment should be to oneself.

Shouldn't it?

Could we have been misled? Could the setting of our course to follow the God of honesty have been a lure to a trap, a deception in the pursuit of self-interest? It seemed like such an honorable thing to do, this truthtelling, even if it meant abandoning civility, because civility is partly built on pretense, and, after all, pretense has no place in an open, honest society. . . .

But it may be that human beings require a form of pretense to make society workable. If I pass you on the street and happen to notice something on your chin, the honest thing to say would be, "Say, that's one hell of an ugly zit you've got there, sport." A simple "Good morning" will probably start everyone's day a bit better, even though, compared to what I was thinking, it would be a pretentiously cordial thing to say. In fact, if you think about it, the transfer of mannerly behavior to children is founded on the ultimate pretense: I was born into this world built to scream for what I want, but if there is to be any order, I need to stop screaming long enough to find out what *you* want. This is not necessarily a natural thing to do: in fact, it is a big pain in the neck for the parent, and frequently a literal pain in the ass for the kid. But, according to tribal wisdom, the common good will be better served by cooperation, and the common good will ultimately preserve the individual.

Is it just possible that in abandoning the pretense that leads to civility we have raised a generation of adults who are still at the cry-baby stage, the "me" generation that would just as soon forego loyalty to a ball club for a few extra megabucks, abandon family for self-expression, or kill a young mother for a joy ride in her car?

I think one big fault we have as a contemporary society is that we put too much faith in what is new; it's easy to do this, since from a technological point of view, what's new is generally improved. But it may be very dangerous to assume this is also true of our social custom; society has evolved on the successes and failures of countless prior generations, and we sometimes don't pay enough attention to this fact. This doesn't mean that we can't improve the way things are, and in many endeavors we have: there is a consciousness there never was before in the areas of race relations, tolerance and respect for the individual. It's just that the benefits of society come at a price, and the biggest chunk of group security was paid for by sacrificing the freedom of the individual to act upon whim, without regard for the common good. We can encourage individual freedom, but with caution, because it is possible the individual will express freedom by compromising the security of the group. When this happens on a grand scale, which isn't too difficult to do in a world shaped by the mass media, the security of the group can be placed in jeopardy.

Somewhere in all this is a message to those of us who cut our teeth on "Leave It to Beaver" and "Father Knows Best." We may have blown one chance to set an example for "Generation X," but who knows? It ain't over 'til the fat lady sings. . . . Just ask Mama Cass.

14.

Perspectives

A wise man was once asked, "If you could be any age, how old would you be?" He thought but a moment, then answered, "Why, exactly as old as I am." This prompted the follow-up question: "How long have you felt this way?" His answer was immediate: "Always, of course!"

The sign of a successful life is the ability to answer that question with the same degree of certitude and conviction as our wise friend. Sure, we all long for times and talents lost, but for every diminishment, there is something gained. We're just not trained to see it, partly because our culture plays heavily to the beauty of youth and the vitality of the physical.

I ask myself what is it I possess now that I was lacking in my youth, for the converse is obvious: it has largely served as the subject of this little book, and if we can take our losses with grace and humor, so much the better. But why on earth would the wise man rather be fifty than thirty?

I think it's because he sees things from a longer view than he used to. He is more tolerant of those whose opinion and style of doing things differ from his. (I think it's for the same reason he's learned to like patchwork quilts: they're just more interesting than color schemes that go together a little too neatly.)

He thinks little kids are really lots of fun to watch, especially when they're interacting with one another, oblivious to the confining convention of an adult world.

He finds it easier to understand his opponent, and because of this, he no longer regards him as such.

He no longer suffers with impatience the coming of spring, because he has learned to enjoy the warmth of the fire and companionship of a good book that winter provides.

He appreciates the virtue of loyalty, for it is a fragile quality undervalued in a me-first world.

He smiles at the arrogance of youth; it's so refreshingly naive.

He is content to pass the baton to his children, for he takes an honest pride in the race he has run.

He no longer fears the dark, for he knows it will soon be dispelled by the sun.

He relishes the crossroad, for it offers the opportunity to express his individuality.

He endures the puffery of the insecure with the compliments that would have obviated the condition.

He has learned to express his talents without modesty, for he understands they are not of his own doing.

He has come to appreciate that in replacing the God of our ignorance, the light of knowledge begins to illuminate His true wisdom.

He has grown comfortable enough with his station in life to enable him to laugh at its glitches and flaws.

Finally, he remains so fascinated by the play of life that he can't wait to see what the next act brings. When the curtain falls, he plans on going backstage to thank the Producer with these words:

"Good show."